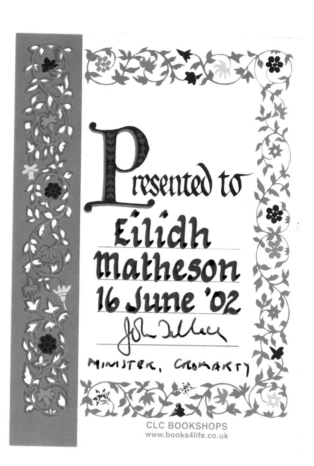

Presented to
Eilidh
Matheson
16 June '02

John Tulloch

MINISTER, CROMARTY

A Child's Book of
Prayers & Graces

Illustrated by Sally Davies

AWARD PUBLICATIONS LIMITED

*For Stephen
and Joel
with love*

ISBN 0-86163-974-X

Copyright © 1999 Award Publications Limited

First published 1999
Second impression 2000

Published by Award Publications Limited,
27 Longford Street, London NW1 3DZ

Printed in Belgium

Father, lead me day by day,
Ever in thine own sweet way;
Teach me to be pure and true,
Show me what I ought to do.

When I'm tempted to do wrong,
Make me steadfast, wise and strong;
And when all alone I stand,
Shield me with thy mighty hand.

When my heart is full of glee,
Help me to remember thee;
Happy most of all to know,
That my Father loves me so.

God bless the master of this house.
God bless the mistress too;
And all the little children
That round the table go.

God bless the food we eat today,
No matter what or come what may!

As I kneel beside my bed
And fold my hands and bow my head,
Dear God, hear this prayer I say:
I want to thank you for today.
Thank you for the sun so bright,
And thank you for the stars tonight;
Thank you for long hours of play;
Thank you for this happy day.

Our Father, who art in heaven,
Hallowed be thy name.
Thy kingdom come.
Thy will be done,
        on earth as it is in heaven.
Give us this day our daily bread.
And forgive us our trespasses,
As we forgive those that
        trespass against us.
And lead us not into temptation;
But deliver us from evil:
For thine is the kingdom,
The power, and the glory,
For ever and ever.

Amen

What can I give Him
Poor as I am?
If I were a shepherd,
I would give a lamb.
If I were a wise man,
I would do my part.
But what can I give Him?
I will give my heart.

God is great,
And God is good,
We thank Him
For this food.

By His hand
Must all be fed:
Thanks be to God
For daily bread.

Jesus bids us shine
With a pure, clear light;
Like a little candle
Burning in the night.
In this world of darkness
We must shine;
You in your small corner
And I in mine.

God be in my head,
    and in my understanding.
God be in mine eyes,
    and in my looking.
God be in my mouth,
    and in my speaking.
God be in my heart,
    and in my thinking.
God be at mine end,
    and at my departing.

Heavenly Father, hear our thanks,
For thy loving care.
Help us now to show our love,
And each blessing share.

I see the moon,
The moon sees me.
God bless the sailors,
And God bless me.

Jesus, tender shepherd,
    hear me;
Bless thy little lambs tonight.
Through the darkness
    be thou near me;
Keep me safe till morning light.

As I lay me down to sleep,
I pray the Lord, my soul to keep;
And in the morning, when I wake,
Please make me good
          for Jesus' sake.

Lord, make me an instrument
   of thy peace;
Where there is hatred,
   let me sow love;
Where there is injury, pardon;
Where there is discord, union;
Where there is doubt, faith;
Where there is despair, hope;
Where there is darkness, light;
Where there is sadness, joy.

You made the trees,
  the flowers, the grass,
The moon and stars,
  the days that pass.
The creatures, great
  and very small.
Dear God – I know
  you made them all.

Praise God from whom
    all blessings flow;
Praise Him, all creatures
    here below;
Praise Him above,
    ye heavenly host;
Praise Father,
      Son and Holy Ghost.

The flower lifts
     its petals up,
And makes its face
     a fragile cup.
Let us give thanks
     for light and air,
And all things that
     show you care.
Dear God, You know
     I want to be,
Grateful for all
     You do for me.
So may my prayer
     this shining hour,
Be lifted to You
     like a flower.

Jesus, bless what thou hast given,
Feed our souls
    with bread from heaven,
Guide and lead us all the way,
In all that we may do and say.

Our hands we fold,
Our heads we bow;
For food and drink
We thank thee now.

Thank you for the world so sweet,
Thank you for the food we eat,
Thank you for the birds that sing;
Thank you, God, for everything.

Matthew, Mark, Luke and John,
Bless the bed that I lie on.
Before I lay me down to sleep,
I give my soul to Christ to keep.
Four corners to my bed,
Four angels there aspread.
One at the head, one at the feet,
And two to guard me while I sleep.

Dear Jesus when I kneel to pray,
Fill my heart with love of You.
And when I meet the coming day,
Guide me in the things I do.

We thank thee heavenly Father,
For every earthly good;
For life and health and clothing,
And for our daily food.

Oh, give us hearts to thank thee,
For every blessing sent;
And whatsoe'er thou sendest,
Make us therewith content.

Dear Lord,
    You are always near me,
Hearing what I say,
Knowing all my thoughts and
        deeds,
All my work and play.

Make me, Lord, obedient, mild,
As becomes a little child.
All day long in every way,
Teach me what to do and say.

Day by day, dear Lord of thee
Three things I pray:
To see thee more clearly,
To love thee more dearly,
To follow thee more nearly,
Day by day.